THE CARE AND KEEPING OF YOU FOR BOYS

(1)

THE ULTIMATE PUBERTY BOOK FOR BOYS

DR. LINDA BROOKIE

The Ultimate Puberty Book for Boys

Copyright © 2023 by:

LINDA BROOKIE

Published in the USA by:

STARLIGHT PUBLICATION

For all the Teenage Boys

To whom we Entrust the Future

CONTENTS

FOREWORD _____

Puberty is a period of significant changes that occur in the body of every boy as they transition from childhood to adulthood. It is a time when they experience physical, emotional, and psychological changes that can be both exciting and confusing. This book is designed to provide boys with a comprehensive guide to puberty, helping them navigate this challenging period with confidence.

The first chapter of this book will introduce boys to the concept of puberty, explaining what it is and why it happens. It will also provide an overview of the different changes that will occur in their bodies during this time, including growth spurts, voice changes, and the development of facial and body hair.

The second chapter will focus on physical changes, including changes in body shape and size, the development of sexual organs, and the emergence of secondary sexual characteristics such as pubic hair and body odor. It will also provide practical advice on personal hygiene and grooming during this time.

The third chapter will address emotional and psychological changes that boys may experience during puberty, including mood swings, changes in self-image, and the development of romantic and sexual feelings. It will also provide tips on coping with these changes and building healthy relationships with peers and family members.

The fourth and final chapter will focus on healthy habits that boys can adopt to support their physical and emotional well-being during puberty. This will include advice on nutrition, exercise, sleep, and stress management.

Throughout the book, boys will find helpful illustrations and real-life examples to help them better understand the changes they are experiencing. By the end of this book, boys will have a better understanding of puberty and the tools they need to navigate this exciting but challenging time with confidence.

Dr. LINDA BROOKIE

Chapter One:

WELCOME TO PUBERTY

Welcome to puberty, boys! This is an exciting but challenging time in your life when you will experience significant changes in your body, mind, and emotions. You may feel excited, scared, or confused, and that's okay. Puberty is a natural and normal part of growing up, and it's important to understand what's happening to you.

During puberty, your body will grow and change, and you will develop into a young adult. You may notice changes in your voice, hair growth, and body shape. You may also experience new emotions and feelings, such as attraction to others.

It's important to remember that everyone goes through puberty at their own pace, and there's no right or wrong way to experience it. It's essential to take care of your body and mind during this time by eating healthy foods, staying active, and getting enough sleep. Most importantly, don't be afraid to talk to trusted adults, such as parents or teachers, about any questions or concerns you may have. Welcome to puberty, boys - it's going to be an exciting journey!

What is Puberty?

Puberty is a natural and normal process of physical, emotional, and psychological changes that occurs as children mature into adults. It is a time of rapid growth and development in which the body undergoes significant changes, including the onset of sexual maturity.

Here are five changes that boys will experience when they go through puberty:

- **Physical changes:** Boys will experience rapid physical growth, which includes an increase in height and weight. They will also experience the development of sexual organs, the growth of facial and body hair, and changes in their voice.

- **Hormonal changes:** During puberty, boys' bodies produce more hormones, including testosterone. This hormone is responsible for the development of male characteristics such as deeper voices, increased muscle mass, and the growth of facial and body hair.

- **Emotional changes:** As boys go through puberty, they may experience mood swings, increased sensitivity to stress, and the development of romantic and sexual feelings.

- **Cognitive changes:** During puberty, boys' brains also undergo significant changes, which can impact their thinking and decision-making abilities.

- **Social changes:** As boys go through puberty, they may experience changes in their relationships with others. They may feel more self-conscious and aware of their bodies, and they may seek out new social connections and experiences.

- **Physical changes:** Boys will notice changes in their body, such as an increase in height and weight, the development of sexual organs, and the growth of facial and body hair.

- **Emotional changes:** Boys may notice changes in their emotions, including mood swings, increased sensitivity to stress, and the development of romantic and sexual feelings.

- **Social changes:** Boys may notice changes in their relationships with others, as they may feel more self-conscious and aware of their bodies. They may seek out new social connections and experiences, and their relationships with family and friends may change as they develop their own identity.

What is Adolescence

Adolescence is the stage of development that marks the transition from childhood to adulthood. It typically begins around the onset of puberty and ends when the individual reaches their mid-20s. Adolescents undergo physical, emotional, and cognitive changes as they mature and begin to establish their identity and independence. They may experience challenges related to social relationships, academic performance, and decision-making, as well as opportunities for personal growth and self-discovery.

How Long Does Puberty Last?

Puberty typically lasts around 2 to 5 years for girls and 3 to 7 years for boys, although the exact duration can vary from person to person. It typically begins between the ages of 8 and 13 for girls and 9 and 14 for boys, and ends around 16 for girls and 18 for boys. During this time, individuals experience physical, emotional, and psychological changes as they transition from childhood to adolescence and eventually into adulthood.

How should I feel about Puberty?

Boys may feel a range of emotions about puberty, including excitement, curiosity, confusion, or anxiety. It is normal to have mixed feelings about the changes that come with puberty. It is important for boys to understand that puberty is a natural and necessary process, and that everyone goes through it at their own pace. Boys should feel empowered to take care of their bodies and minds during this time by eating healthy foods, staying active, and getting enough rest. They should also know that it is okay to seek help from trusted adults, such as parents, teachers, or healthcare providers, if they have any questions or concerns. With support and understanding, boys can navigate through the changes of puberty with confidence and a positive attitude.

During puberty, boys may feel uncertain about the changes they are experiencing, especially if they feel like they are not developing as quickly as their peers. It is important for boys to understand that everyone goes through puberty at their own pace, and that there is no "right" or "wrong" way to develop. Boys should also be encouraged to express their feelings and concerns to trusted adults, who can provide guidance and support during this time. It is important to provide boys with accurate and age-appropriate information about puberty so that they can better understand the changes happening to their bodies and minds. With this knowledge, boys can take an active role in their own development and make healthy choices that support their overall well-being.

Why will my Feelings Change During Puberty?

During puberty, a boy's feelings may change due to a combination of physical, hormonal, and social factors. The physical changes that occur during puberty, such as growth spurts and the development of sexual organs, can affect a boy's self-image and confidence. Hormonal changes, particularly the increase in testosterone, can also impact a boy's mood, making him more irritable, impulsive, or emotional. Social changes, such as the desire for greater independence and the development of new friendships and romantic relationships, can further contribute to a boy's changing emotions. It is important to recognize that these changes are a normal part of puberty and that with support and understanding, boys can navigate through this stage of development with greater confidence and resilience.

During puberty, boys experience a variety of physical, emotional, and social changes that can impact their feelings and behavior. Physically, boys undergo a rapid period of growth and development, with their bodies changing in size, shape, and appearance. They may experience acne, body hair growth, and changes in their voice, which can affect their self-image and confidence.

Hormonal changes also play a key role in shaping a boy's emotions during puberty. As testosterone levels increase, boys may experience a range of feelings, including irritability, mood swings, and increased sensitivity to stress. These hormonal fluctuations can also cause changes in sexual desire and attraction, leading to new feelings and curiosities around romantic and sexual relationships.

Social changes during puberty can also affect a boy's emotions, as they begin to establish greater independence and develop new friendships and relationships outside of their family. Boys may feel pressure to conform to social norms and expectations, which can cause stress and anxiety. At the same time, they may also feel excited and curious about the new experiences and opportunities that come with this stage of development.

It is important for boys to receive accurate and age-appropriate information about puberty so that they can better understand the changes happening to their bodies and minds. Parents, teachers, and healthcare providers can play a critical role in providing this support and guidance, answering questions, and helping boys navigate through the challenges and opportunities of puberty.

Boys should also be encouraged to express their feelings and concerns, and to seek help and support when needed. By talking openly about their emotions and experiences, boys can develop greater self-awareness and emotional intelligence, which can help them build stronger relationships and cope with stress and challenges throughout their lives. With support and understanding, boys can embrace the changes of puberty with confidence and resilience, and emerge stronger and more self-assured on the other side.

Here are five ideas for making a difference:

- **Provide accurate information:** It is important to provide boys with accurate and age-appropriate information about puberty. This includes information about the physical changes that occur during puberty, as well as the emotional and social changes that come with this stage of development.
- **Encourage healthy habits:** Boys should be encouraged to develop healthy habits, such as eating a balanced diet, getting enough exercise

and sleep, and avoiding harmful substances like tobacco and drugs. These habits can support their overall physical and mental health during puberty and beyond.

- **Foster open communication:** Encourage boys to talk openly and honestly about their feelings and experiences during puberty. Provide a safe and non-judgmental environment for boys to ask questions and seek guidance.

- **Promote positive self-image:** Help boys build a positive self-image by focusing on their strengths and accomplishments, rather than their physical appearance. Encourage them to develop their interests and hobbies, and to pursue activities that bring them joy and fulfillment.

- **Address toxic masculinity:** Challenge toxic masculinity by promoting positive messages about masculinity and encouraging boys to reject harmful stereotypes and expectations. Teach them to respect and value the feelings and experiences of others, and to prioritize healthy relationships and communication.

Why do I care more about what I look like? I never used to think about it.

During puberty, a boy's physical appearance can become an important aspect of his identity and self-image. As their bodies undergo rapid changes, boys may become more self-conscious about their appearance and feel pressure to conform to social norms and expectations.

Furthermore, during puberty, boys begin to form new friendships and romantic relationships, and their physical appearance can play a role in attracting others and forming connections. Boys may feel pressure to present themselves in a certain way to be perceived as attractive or desirable.

In addition, physical appearance can also impact a boy's confidence and self-esteem, which can in turn affect his overall well-being and mental health. It is important for boys to develop a positive self-image and to feel comfortable in their own skin, regardless of societal expectations or pressures.

Parents, caregivers, and educators can help boys navigate these challenges by providing support and guidance, promoting positive messages about body image and self-worth, and encouraging boys to focus on their strengths and accomplishments rather than their appearance.

"Embrace the changes of puberty with confidence, knowing that you are growing and evolving into the best version of yourself."

What is happening to my voice lately? One minute it sounds squeaky and the next it sounds so deep.

During puberty, a boy's larynx, or voice box, undergoes significant changes that can affect the sound and tone of his voice. As testosterone levels increase, the vocal cords thicken and lengthen, causing the voice to deepen and become more resonant. This process, known as voice breaking, can be gradual or sudden, and may cause some boys to feel self-conscious or embarrassed about the changes in their voice. However, it is a natural and normal part of puberty, and typically occurs between the ages of 12 and 16. With time and practice, most boys learn to adjust to their new voice and embrace their unique sound, which can be an important aspect of their developing identity and self-expression.

The voice box, or larynx, plays a crucial role in the development of an adolescent boy's voice during puberty. As hormones trigger growth and thickening of the vocal cords, the voice may crack or break, leading to temporary or permanent changes in tone and pitch.

With time and practice, most boys learn to adjust to their new voice and embrace the unique sound that comes with this stage of development.

Here are some questions and answers that may bother boys during puberty:

Q: Why is my voice cracking?

A: Your voice is cracking because your vocal cords are growing and thickening, causing your voice to deepen and become more resonant. This is a normal part of puberty.

Q: Why am I growing hair in new places?

A: As testosterone levels increase during puberty, hair may begin to grow in new places, such as on the face, chest, and pubic area. This is a natural and normal part of puberty.

Q: Why am I getting acne?

A: Hormonal changes during puberty can cause an increase in oil production, leading to clogged pores and acne. Keeping your skin clean and avoiding touching your face can help manage acne.

Q: Why do I feel so self-conscious about my body?

A: It's common to feel self-conscious about your body during puberty as it undergoes rapid changes. Remember that everyone's body develops differently and focus on developing a positive self-image.

Q: How can I manage my changing emotions?

A: Emotions can be intense and overwhelming during puberty. Practice self-care, such as getting enough sleep and exercise, and seek support from friends, family, or a mental health professional if needed.

Chapter Two:

WET DREAMS AND ERECTIONS

Wet dreams, also known as nocturnal emissions, can be a confusing and sometimes embarrassing experience for boys going through puberty. These spontaneous orgasms that occur during sleep can feel scary or strange, but they are a normal part of sexual development. In this chapter, we will explore the science behind wet dreams, the reasons they happen, and how to manage the physical and emotional aspects of this experience. By understanding wet dreams and learning how to navigate them, boys can approach this aspect of puberty with confidence and self-assurance.

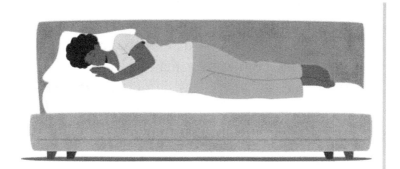

Why do I get erections?

Boys get an erection when blood flow increases to the penis, causing it to become hard and erect. This happens as a result of sexual stimulation, such as physical touch, visual or auditory cues, or sexual thoughts and fantasies. When the brain receives signals of sexual arousal, it triggers the release of hormones that cause the muscles in the penis to relax and blood vessels to dilate, allowing more blood to flow into the penis. This increased blood flow causes the penis to expand and become firm. Erections can happen spontaneously or in response to sexual stimulation, and they are a normal and healthy part of male sexual function.

Erections are a natural and necessary part of male sexual function. They occur when blood flow increases to the penis, causing it to become hard and erect. Sexual stimulation, such as physical touch, visual or auditory cues, or sexual thoughts and fantasies, can trigger an erection by signaling the brain to release hormones that relax the muscles in the penis and increase blood flow to the area. Erections can happen spontaneously or in response to sexual stimulation, and they are important for sexual intercourse and other sexual activities. While they may feel embarrassing or uncomfortable at times, it's important for boys to understand that erections are a normal and healthy part of sexual development and should be embraced and celebrated as such.

What do I do when I get an erection in an embarrassing situation, like in class?

If a boy gets an erection in an embarrassing situation, like in class, the best thing to do is to try to conceal it discreetly. They can cross their legs or adjust their position to make it less noticeable. They can also try to focus their thoughts on something non-sexual, such as a school assignment or a hobby. It's important for boys to remember that erections are a natural and normal bodily response and are nothing to be ashamed of. If the erection persists or becomes uncomfortable, it may be appropriate to excuse oneself to go to the restroom until it subsides. It's also important for boys to talk to a trusted adult, such as a parent or healthcare provider, about any concerns or questions they have about their sexual development.

What is ejaculation?

Ejaculation is the release of semen from the penis during sexual activity. It occurs when the muscles in the reproductive system contract and force semen out of the penis. Semen is a fluid that contains sperm and other substances that nourish and protect them. Ejaculation is a natural and necessary part of male sexual function, and it typically happens during orgasm.

There are two types of ejaculation: nocturnal emission (also known as a "wet dream") and intentional ejaculation during sexual activity. Nocturnal emissions occur during sleep and are often a normal part of puberty. Intentional ejaculation can happen during masturbation or sexual intercourse.

Ejaculation can be accompanied by intense physical and emotional sensations, and it is a pleasurable experience for many men. However, it can also be accompanied by feelings of shame, embarrassment, or guilt for some individuals. It's important for boys to understand that ejaculation is a normal and healthy part of male sexual function and should be embraced and celebrated as such.

It's also important for boys to understand that ejaculation can result in the transmission of sexually transmitted infections (STIs) and unwanted pregnancy. Using barrier methods of contraception, such as condoms, can reduce the risk of STI transmission and unintended pregnancy.

When will I ejaculate for the first time?

Boys typically experience their first ejaculation during puberty, which usually occurs between the ages of 9 and 14. This is a normal and natural part of sexual development and may occur during masturbation or sexual activity. The timing of a boy's first ejaculation can vary and may be influenced by genetics, environment, and other factors. It's important for boys to understand that ejaculation is a normal and healthy part of sexual development and should be celebrated as such. They should also be educated on safe sexual practices to protect themselves and their partners.

Sometimes I wake up with sticky pajamas. What happened?

Waking up with sticky pajamas can be a result of a nocturnal emission, also known as a "wet dream." Wet dreams are a normal and natural part of male sexual development and can occur during puberty and beyond. They happen when the body releases semen during sleep, typically during a dream. Boys may feel embarrassed or ashamed when they experience a wet dream, but it's important for them to understand that it's a normal bodily function and nothing to be ashamed of.

I hear some kids talking about blue balls. What's that?

Blue balls is a slang term for the uncomfortable or painful sensation that some males may experience in their testicles after sexual arousal without ejaculation. The condition is caused by an increased blood flow to the genitals during arousal, which can cause swelling and pressure. While blue balls can be uncomfortable, it is not a serious medical condition and typically resolves on its own after ejaculation or after a period of time. It's important for boys to understand that blue balls can be alleviated by engaging in sexual activity, masturbating, or simply waiting for the discomfort to subside.

What is masturbation?

Masturbation is a form of sexual stimulation that involves touching or rubbing one's own genitals for sexual pleasure. It is a normal and healthy part of sexual development and can be a way for individuals to explore their own bodies and learn about their own sexual preferences. Masturbation is a safe and private activity and does not typically lead to any negative physical or emotional consequences. It's important for individuals to understand that masturbation is a personal choice and there is no right or wrong way to engage in this activity.

"Masturbation is a natural and healthy expression of sexuality, and there's no shame in exploring and enjoying your own body."

It's important for individuals to understand that masturbation is a personal choice and should only be engaged in when one feels comfortable and ready to do so. Masturbation can provide a safe and healthy outlet for sexual desires and can also help relieve stress and improve overall well-being. It's important for individuals to practice good hygiene and to always respect their own boundaries and limitations when engaging in this activity.

MYTHBUSTERS

- ➢ Masturbation can cause blindness or other physical problems.
- ➢ Masturbation is only for people who can't find a partner or who are lonely.
- ➢ Masturbation is a sin or immoral act.
- ➢ Masturbation can lead to infertility or reduced sexual sensitivity.

Can masturbating do anything bad to me? Is it possible to masturbate too much?

Like with many activities, it is possible for someone to engage in masturbation too frequently or excessively. This can potentially lead to physical irritation or soreness in the genital area, as well as emotional or mental fatigue. However, what is considered "too much" varies from person to person and depends on individual circumstances. It is important for individuals to listen to their bodies and recognize when they may be engaging in masturbation too frequently, and to take breaks or seek professional help if needed.

Chapter Three:

RELATIONSHIPS

Relationships can be both exciting and confusing for boys during puberty. As they navigate the changes happening in their bodies and minds, they may also start to explore new feelings towards others. It's important for boys to understand the different types of relationships and how to build healthy connections with others, while also respecting boundaries and practicing communication skills. This chapter will explore the various aspects of relationships during puberty, including romantic relationships, friendships, and family dynamics.

What makes a good friend?

A good friend is someone who is trustworthy, supportive, and respectful. They are someone who is there for you when you need them, and they listen to you without judgment. Good friends are honest with each other and are able to communicate openly and effectively. They are also reliable and dependable, keeping their promises and showing up when they say they will. A good friend is someone who accepts you for who you are, and doesn't try to change you. They celebrate your successes and offer a shoulder to lean on during tough times. Ultimately, a good friend is someone who enriches your life and makes it more fulfilling.

What makes a good friend?

Making a good friend requires effort and the ability to

be open and approachable. One way to make friends is to get involved in activities that interest you. This can include joining a sports team, club, or volunteering in your community. When you meet someone new, be yourself and show interest in what they have to say. Listen actively, ask questions, and share your own experiences. Respect their boundaries and be trustworthy by keeping their secrets and not betraying their trust. Communication is key in any relationship, so make sure to express yourself clearly and listen actively to their responses. Remember, it takes time to build a strong friendship, so be patient and keep investing in the relationship.

How do I keep a good friend?

To maintain a good friendship during puberty, a boy should continue to show interest in his friend's life, listen to their thoughts and feelings, and communicate openly and honestly. It's important to be supportive, respect each other's boundaries, and trust each other. Regularly spending time together can help strengthen the bond, whether it's through shared hobbies or simply hanging out. It's also important to apologize and make amends when mistakes are made or conflicts arise. Boys experiencing puberty may be going through a lot of changes and emotions, but it's important to remember that good friendships can provide a sense of support, comfort, and fun during this time.

What should I do when I'm arguing with a friend?

Arguments and conflicts can arise in any friendship, and it's important to know how to handle them in a constructive way.

Here are some tips for what to do when you're arguing with a friend:

- *Take a deep breath and remain calm. It's easy to get caught up in the heat of the moment and say things you'll regret later. Try to take a step back and calm down before continuing the conversation.*
- *Listen to your friend's point of view. Even if you don't agree with them, it's important to hear them out and try to understand where they're coming from.*
- *Express your own feelings in a clear and respectful manner. Use "I" statements instead of "you" statements, which can come across as accusatory.*
- *Find common ground. Even if you don't agree on everything, there may be some points of agreement that you can build on.*
- *Look for solutions together. Instead of focusing on who is right or wrong, work together to find a solution that satisfies both of you.*
- *Apologize when necessary. If you said or did something hurtful, it's important to take*

responsibility for your actions and apologize sincerely.

- *Forgive and move on. Holding a grudge will only make the situation worse. Once the argument is resolved, try to let it go and focus on rebuilding your friendship.*

It's important to remember that arguments and conflicts are a normal part of any relationship, and can even be an opportunity for growth and strengthening your bond. By handling them in a constructive way, you can build trust, respect, and understanding with your friend.

What do I do if an argument is about to turn physical?

When an argument is about to turn physical, it's important to try and defuse the situation as quickly as possible. First, try to take a step back and take a deep breath. It's crucial to remain calm and avoid getting drawn into a physical confrontation. If you feel threatened, try to remove yourself from the situation and find a safe place.

- *If you can't leave, try to de-escalate the situation by using words. Try to understand the other person's perspective and express your own calmly and respectfully. It's also important to listen actively and avoid interrupting.*

- *If things still escalate, seek help from a trusted adult, such as a parent, teacher, or counselor. It's better to involve an adult than to try and handle the situation alone. Remember, physical violence is never the answer and can lead to serious consequences.*

- *After the situation has been resolved, it's important to reflect on what happened and learn from it. This will help prevent similar situations from occurring in the future and allow you to maintain a healthy and positive relationship with your friend.*

What happens if my good friend and I are growing apart?

As you go through puberty, it's common to experience changes in your friendships. Sometimes, it may feel like you and your good friend are growing apart. This can be a difficult experience, but it's a normal part of growing up.

If you're feeling like your friendship is changing, try talking to your friend about how you're feeling. Be honest and open about your concerns. You may find that your friend is feeling the same way, and you can work together to find ways to reconnect.

If you find that your interests and activities are changing and you no longer have as much in common with your friend, it's okay to explore new friendships. You don't have to completely end the friendship, but you can give each other space to grow and pursue your own interests.

Remember that friendships naturally ebb and flow, and it's okay to let go of friendships that no longer serve you. It's also okay to invest time and energy in new friendships that align with your current interests and values. Just be sure to treat your old friend with kindness and respect, even if you're no longer as close as you used to be.

We're in middle school, but one of my friends acts like he's still in elementary school!

It can be tough when friends start to mature at different rates. If you notice that one of your friends is still acting like they're in elementary school, it's important to approach the situation with kindness and empathy. Try to talk to your friend privately and ask them if everything is okay. Perhaps they're going through something that is making them act out. If they don't want to talk, it's important to be patient and understanding. You don't want to make them feel embarrassed or ashamed for acting differently than you.

It's also important to set boundaries and communicate your needs. If your friend's behavior is bothering you or causing problems, it's okay to tell them how you feel. You can do this in a kind and respectful way, without attacking or blaming them. Remember, friendships can go through ups and downs, but with open communication and mutual respect, you can work through any challenges that come your way.

What is a clique?

A clique is a social group consisting of individuals who share common interests, attitudes, and behaviors. It is a group that tends to exclude outsiders and only allows people who are similar to them to join. Cliques often form during adolescence, when young people are trying to establish their identity and find a sense of belonging.

Cliques can have positive or negative effects on the individuals who are part of them. Positive cliques can provide a sense of belonging and support for its members, while negative cliques can lead to exclusion and bullying of outsiders. Negative cliques can also lead to conformity and pressure to engage in risky behaviors, such as substance abuse or reckless driving.

It is important to note that not all groups of friends are cliques. A group of friends can be inclusive and accepting of others who share their interests, without excluding those who don't. However, if a group of friends is exclusionary and only allows people who are similar to them to join, then it may be considered a clique.

I keep hearing about peer pressure. What is it?

Peer pressure refers to the influence that peers, or friends, can have on an individual's behavior or decisions. This can be both positive and negative, as friends may encourage someone to participate in activities that are good for them, or they may pressure them into engaging in risky or harmful behavior.

Positive peer pressure can encourage individuals to make good decisions and can help build self-confidence and social skills. For example, if a friend encourages someone to join a sports team or a school club, it can help them make new friends and develop new skills.

Negative peer pressure, on the other hand, can lead to unhealthy behavior, such as drug or alcohol abuse, bullying, or skipping school. In some cases, peer pressure can even result in criminal activity.

Peer pressure can come in different forms, such as direct pressure, where someone is directly urged to do something, or indirect pressure, where someone feels pressure to fit in with a group. It can also be overt or covert, with overt pressure being obvious and direct, while covert pressure is subtle and indirect.

It is important for adolescents to learn how to navigate peer pressure and make their own decisions. This can involve setting boundaries, standing up for oneself, and choosing friends who have similar values and interests. It can also involve seeking help from a trusted adult if they feel uncomfortable or pressured in a situation.

Overall, peer pressure can have a significant impact on an individual's development and choices during adolescence. It is important to understand the dynamics of peer pressure and how to resist negative influence in order to make healthy and responsible decisions.

"Your choice of friends can make or break you. Choose wisely, and you'll soar; choose poorly, and you'll stumble."

Some of my friends have started shoplifting. They keep asking me to do it with them but I don't want to. What should I do?

It's important to stand up for what you believe in, even if it means going against the group. Shoplifting is illegal and can have serious consequences. It's okay to say no and to distance yourself from friends who engage in illegal activities. You can also talk to a trusted adult, such as a parent, teacher, or counselor, about the situation and ask for their advice. Sometimes, peer pressure can be overwhelming and it's okay to seek help. If your friends continue to pressure you, it may be necessary to cut ties with them and find new friends who share your values and beliefs. Remember, your actions and choices are your own and it's important to make decisions that align with your personal values and morals, even if it means going against the crowd.

What should I do if my friends are trying to get me to try using drugs, alcohol, or cigarettes?

If your friends are pressuring you to try drugs, alcohol, or cigarettes, it's essential to remember that you have the power to say no. It can be challenging to stand up to your friends, but it's essential to prioritize your health and safety.

First, it's helpful to understand why your friends might be pressuring you to try these substances. They may be seeking validation or trying to fit in with a particular group. They may also be dealing with their stress or using substances as a coping mechanism.

To avoid the situation, you can try changing the subject, suggesting other activities to do, or simply saying no. It's okay to set boundaries with your friends and make it clear that you're not comfortable with their behavior.

If your friends persist in pressuring you, it might be time to re-evaluate your friendship. Good friends will respect your choices and boundaries, even if they don't agree with them. If your friends continue to pressure you, it may be time to seek support from a trusted adult, such as a parent, teacher, or counselor.

Remember that the consequences of using drugs, alcohol, or cigarettes can be severe, including addiction, health problems, and legal trouble. It's crucial to make informed decisions about your health and safety.

If you're struggling with peer pressure or substance use, there are resources available to help you. Consider reaching out to a support group or seeking guidance from a mental health professional. Remember that you're not alone, and there is help available.

What if I'm thinking about trying drinking or smoking, like some of my friends?

It's natural to be curious about things that your friends are doing, especially if you're feeling left out or want to fit in. However, it's important to understand that alcohol, smoking, and drugs can have serious negative effects on your health and well-being.

Before making any decisions, it's important to educate yourself about the risks and consequences of these behaviors. Talk to a trusted adult, such as a parent, teacher, or school counselor, to get more information and support.

If you decide that you don't want to try drinking, smoking, or drugs, it's important to be assertive and say no when your friends offer. You can say something like,

"No thanks, I don't want to try that" or "I don't think that's a good idea."

It's also important to surround yourself with friends who support your decision to stay away from these behaviors. Seek out friends who share your interests and values, and who respect your choices.

If you're feeling pressured or uncomfortable in a situation, it's okay to remove yourself from it. You can say something like, "I'm not comfortable with this, I'm going to go home" or "I don't want to be part of this, I'm going to hang out with other friends."

Remember that your health and well-being are important, and it's okay to prioritize them over fitting in with a certain group of friends. Making smart choices now can help set you up for a healthy and happy future.

What is Bullying?

Bullying is a form of aggressive behavior that is intentionally harmful, repeated, and involves an imbalance of power between the bully and the victim. It can take many forms, including physical, verbal, social, and cyberbullying. Physical bullying involves hitting, kicking, pushing, or other acts of physical aggression. Verbal bullying involves name-calling, teasing, or insults. Social bullying involves excluding or isolating someone from a group or spreading rumors about them. Cyberbullying involves using electronic devices or social media platforms to harass, threaten, or embarrass someone.

What do I do if I am being bullied?

Bullying can have serious consequences for both the victim and the bully. Victims of bullying may experience anxiety, depression, and low self-esteem. They may also have trouble concentrating in school, experience physical health problems, and even contemplate or attempt suicide. Bullies, on the other hand, may have difficulty forming healthy relationships, struggle with substance abuse, and engage in criminal behavior later in life.

It is important for individuals to recognize the signs of bullying and to take action if they witness or experience it. This may involve reporting the behavior to a teacher or other authority figure, seeking support from friends and family, or reaching out to counseling services for help. It is also essential to create a culture of respect and kindness in schools, communities, and online spaces to prevent bullying from occurring in the first place.

Bullying can have serious effects on a person's mental health and self-esteem. It can cause feelings of anxiety, depression, and hopelessness. Victims of bullying may also experience physical symptoms such as stomachaches and headaches. Bullying can take many forms, including physical, verbal, and cyberbullying. It often involves a power imbalance, with the bully exerting control over the victim. It is important to recognize the signs of bullying and take action to prevent it. Adults can help by creating a safe and supportive environment for children and intervening when they see bullying behavior. It is important for victims to speak up and seek help, as well as for bystanders to stand up for what is right and support their peers.

If you're being bullied, there are several things you can do. First, it's important to tell someone you trust, such as a parent, teacher, or school counselor. They can help you come up with a plan to address the situation. You can also try to avoid the bully and stay with a group of friends when possible. It's important not to retaliate or fight back, as this can often make the situation worse. You should also try to stay calm and confident, and remember that the bullying is not your fault. Finally, if the bullying continues, you may need to seek additional help or involve authorities, such as school administrators or law enforcement.

What do I do if a friend is being bullied?

If you see a friend being bullied, it's important to take action and help them. You can start by telling the bully to stop and that their behavior is not okay. If that doesn't work, try getting an adult involved, like a teacher, coach, or parent. Make sure your friend knows that they're not alone and that you're there to support them. Encourage them to talk about what happened and how it made them feel. Sometimes, just being there to listen can make a big difference. Let them know that you believe in them and that they deserve to be treated with respect. Remember, standing up to bullies is not just the right thing to do, it's also brave and shows true strength of character.

Is it possible that I am a bully?

Yes, it is possible for anyone to become a bully, even unintentionally. Sometimes, bullying behavior can stem from a lack of understanding or empathy towards others. It can also be a result of peer pressure or the desire to fit in with a particular group. It is important to recognize if you are exhibiting bullying behavior, and to take steps to change that behavior. This can include seeking help from a trusted adult or counselor, practicing empathy and kindness towards others, and being aware of the impact your actions have on those around you. It is never too late to make a change and become a better person, and acknowledging that you may have acted as a bully in the past is the first step towards that change.

Chapter Four:

YOUR FEELINGS

As boys go through puberty, they experience a wide range of emotions and feelings that may be new or intense. It can be challenging to navigate these feelings, especially when they are not familiar with them. In this chapter, we will explore different types of emotions and feelings that boys may experience during this period of their lives. We will discuss how to identify and express these emotions in a healthy way, and how to cope with difficult or overwhelming feelings. We will also touch upon the importance of seeking support and talking to trusted adults or friends when needed. By understanding and managing their emotions, boys can develop better self-awareness and resilience, which can help them navigate challenges and build stronger relationships with others.

Why do my feelings seem to be changing so much lately?

During puberty, your body is going through many physical and hormonal changes. This can lead to fluctuations in your emotions and moods. Hormones, such as testosterone and estrogen, play a significant role in regulating your mood, energy levels, and emotions. As the levels of these hormones change during puberty, you may experience mood swings, feel easily overwhelmed, or have trouble controlling your emotions. These changes can also be influenced by external factors, such as social pressures, academic stress, and family issues. It is essential to remember that these emotional changes are normal and expected during puberty.

It is crucial to find healthy ways to manage your emotions and cope with any stressors you may be facing. Talking to a trusted adult, practicing self-care, and engaging in healthy activities such as exercise and hobbies can help you navigate these changes and improve your emotional well-being.

I sometimes feel bad about myself. Why?

It's normal to feel bad about yourself from time to time, especially during puberty when you're going through many physical and emotional changes. You might compare yourself to others, feel like you're not good at something, or worry about how others perceive you. These negative feelings can also be influenced by factors like stress, lack of sleep, or changes in hormones. It's important to remember that everyone has negative feelings about themselves at times, but it's important to take care of your mental health by talking to someone you trust, practicing self-care, and reminding yourself of your strengths and accomplishments.

What can I do to feel better about myself?

Feeling good about oneself is an essential part of emotional well-being during puberty.

Here are some tips that can help you feel better about yourself:

- *Focus on your positive qualities: Everyone has positive qualities. Focus on them and remind yourself of them often.*
- *Be kind to yourself: Speak to yourself the way you would speak to a friend. Treat yourself with kindness and compassion.*
- *Set goals and work towards them: Set goals that you can realistically achieve and work towards them. Accomplishing something can boost your self-esteem.*
- *Surround yourself with positive people: Being around positive, supportive people can help you feel better about yourself.*
- *Practice self-care: Taking care of yourself can make you feel better physically and mentally. Eat healthy, get enough sleep, and exercise regularly.*
- *Seek help if needed: If you are struggling with feelings of low self-esteem or have concerns about your mental health, seek help from a trusted adult or a mental health professional.*

Remember, feeling good about yourself is a process, and it takes time and effort. But by taking small steps, you can improve your self-esteem and overall well-being.

It sometimes seems that my parents don't understand me anymore. Why?

As you go through puberty, you may feel like your parents don't understand you as much as they used to. This can be frustrating and confusing, but it's a common experience for many teenagers. Part of the reason for this may be that you are going through a lot of changes, both physical and emotional, and it can be hard for your parents to keep up.

Additionally, your parents may have their own stressors and worries that they are dealing with, which can make it difficult for them to focus on your needs. It's important to remember that your parents still care about you, even if they don't always show it in the way you want them to. They may be struggling to adapt to your changing needs and behaviors, but it's important to communicate with them and try to understand where they're coming from.

How can I get my parents to listen to me?

One way to improve your relationship with your parents is to have open and honest conversations with them. Share your thoughts and feelings with them and listen to their perspective as well. Remember that they were once teenagers too and may have gone through similar experiences. It's also important to try to be patient and understanding with them, even if it's difficult at times. With time and effort, you can build a stronger relationship with your parents and feel more understood.

It is common to experience feelings of anger during puberty due to the hormonal changes and increased stress levels. It is important to know how to manage anger in a healthy way to prevent it from turning into aggression or causing harm to oneself or others.

What should I do when I'm feeling angry?

The first step to managing anger is to recognize when it is starting to build up. Common physical signs include increased heart rate, muscle tension, and feeling hot or flushed. Once you have identified that you are feeling angry, take a step back and try to calm yourself down. This can be achieved through deep breathing, counting to ten, or finding a physical outlet like exercise or punching a pillow.

It is also important to understand the root cause of your anger. Is it something that can be addressed and resolved through communication with the person or situation involved? Or is it a deeper, ongoing issue that requires therapy or counseling? Identifying the root cause can help you develop a plan for managing and resolving your anger.

Another helpful technique is to practice positive self-talk. This involves reminding yourself of your strengths and abilities, as well as using affirmations to reinforce positive thinking patterns. It can also be helpful to practice empathy and try to see the situation from another person's perspective.

Finally, it is important to seek support from others. This can include talking to a trusted friend or family member, joining a support group, or seeking professional help from a therapist or counselor. Talking through your feelings with others can help you gain perspective and develop coping strategies for managing your anger.

Remember, it is normal to experience feelings of anger, but it is important to manage them in a healthy and constructive way. With practice and support, you can learn to manage your anger and maintain positive relationships with others.

Feeling shy around others is common, and it's okay to feel that way. However, if you feel like your shyness is interfering with your ability to make friends or enjoy social situations, there are things you can do to help yourself.

I wish I felt more comfortable around people. What can I do about being shy?

One way to become more comfortable around people is to start small. For example, you might try striking up a conversation with someone you don't know well, or attending a social event with a friend who can help you feel more comfortable. You can also practice basic social skills, such as making eye contact, smiling, and asking questions to show you're interested in what others have to say.

Another way to overcome shyness is to challenge yourself to do things that make you feel uncomfortable. This could mean volunteering for a group project, signing up for a club or activity, or trying something new that pushes you outside your comfort zone. Remember, the more you practice being social, the easier it will become.

It's also important to be patient with yourself. Overcoming shyness takes time, and it's okay to make mistakes or feel awkward sometimes. Just keep practicing, and don't be too hard on yourself if things don't go perfectly. With time and effort, you can become more comfortable around people and enjoy social situations more.

Lately I've been feeling stressed out. What can I do about it?

If you've been feeling stressed out lately, there are a few things you can try to help manage your stress. First, take a deep breath and try to relax. You may want to try a relaxation technique like deep breathing or progressive muscle relaxation. Exercise can also be a great way to reduce stress and improve your mood. Additionally, make sure you're getting enough sleep and eating a healthy diet, as both can affect your mood and stress levels.

Another important step in managing stress is to identify the source of your stress and try to address it. This may involve making changes to your schedule, avoiding certain situations or people that trigger your stress, or seeking support from friends or family.

If your stress is overwhelming or persistent, it may be helpful to speak with a mental health professional, who can provide you with additional strategies for managing your stress and improving your overall well-being. Remember, it's okay to ask for help when you need it.

Sometimes I feel really unhappy. Should I be worried?
Feeling unhappy from time to time is a normal part of life. It is natural to experience sadness, disappointment, and other negative emotions. However, if these feelings persist for a long time and start to affect your daily life, then it is time to take action.

It is important to understand that feeling unhappy is not a sign of weakness or failure. Everyone experiences ups and downs, and it is perfectly okay to ask for help. Talking to a trusted friend or family member can be a good first step. They may be able to provide support, advice, or simply a listening ear.

If you find that your unhappiness is becoming overwhelming or difficult to manage, it may be helpful to speak to a mental health professional such as a counselor or therapist. They can help you explore the reasons behind your feelings and provide tools and strategies to help you cope.

It is also important to take care of your physical health when dealing with feelings of unhappiness. Getting enough sleep, eating a healthy diet, and engaging in regular exercise can help improve your mood and overall well-being.

Remember that it is okay to feel unhappy, and it is important to take steps to address these feelings. Seeking support from trusted individuals and professionals can help you navigate this difficult time and move towards a happier, healthier life.

My grandfather recently died and I'm confused about what I'm feeling.

Losing someone close to us, such as a grandparent, can be a very difficult and confusing time. It is normal to experience a range of emotions during the grieving process, and it is important to acknowledge and accept these emotions rather than suppressing them.

You may feel sad, angry, guilty, or even relieved. All of these emotions are normal, and it is important to remember that everyone experiences grief differently. Don't feel pressured to feel a certain way or to follow a specific timeline for your grief.

It's also important to take care of yourself during this time. Try to maintain a healthy routine with enough sleep, exercise, and healthy food. Consider talking to someone you trust, such as a family member, friend, or counselor, about your feelings. They may be able to provide comfort and support during this difficult time.

If you find that your grief is affecting your daily life and activities for an extended period of time, or if you are having thoughts of self-harm or suicide, seek help from a mental health professional immediately. They can provide you with the support and resources you need to cope with your grief and move forward. Remember, grieving is a process, and healing takes time.

I recently found out that my parents are separating. What can I do?

Finding out that your parents are separating can be a difficult and confusing time for anyone. It's important to remember that it's not your fault and that your parents still love you. Here are some things you can do:

- **Talk to someone you trust:** This could be a friend, family member, or even a counselor. It can be helpful to talk about your feelings and get support.
- **Take care of yourself:** Make sure you are eating well, getting enough sleep, and exercising. Take time to do things you enjoy and that make you feel good.

- **Ask your parents questions:** You may have a lot of questions about what's happening and why. Ask your parents for answers and try to have an open and honest conversation.
- **Don't take sides:** It's important to remember that your parents' separation is between them and has nothing to do with you. Don't feel like you have to take sides or choose between them.
- **Seek professional help:** If you're feeling really overwhelmed, it can be helpful to talk to a therapist or counselor who can help you process your feelings and provide support during this difficult time.

Remember, it's okay to feel sad or upset, but things will get better over time. Just make sure you take care of yourself and seek help if you need it.

Believe in yourself, be kind to others, and never give up on your dreams. Always strive to learn, grow, and make a positive impact in the world.

I feel weird talking about my feelings.

It's understandable to feel uncomfortable about discussing your emotions. However, it's important to remember that talking about your feelings can help you better understand and manage them. Consider reaching out to a trusted friend or family member, a therapist, or a counselor to talk through your emotions. You don't have to go through difficult times alone.

Why is it important to talk about your feelings?

Answer: Talking about your feelings can help you process and understand them better. It can also help you feel more connected to others and build stronger relationships.

Who can I talk to about my feelings?

Answer: You can talk to anyone you trust, such as a friend, family member, teacher, or counselor. There are also hotlines and online resources available for those who need to talk to someone anonymously.

What if I don't feel comfortable talking about my feelings?

Answer: It's okay to take your time and find a way to express your feelings that feels comfortable to you. You can try writing in a journal, drawing, or even talking to a pet or stuffed animal.

How can I tell if someone else is struggling with their emotions?

Answer: Look for signs such as changes in behavior or mood, withdrawal from social activities, or expressing feelings of sadness or hopelessness. If you're concerned about someone, it's important to talk to them and offer support.

Is it okay to cry?

Answer: Yes, it's okay to cry. Crying can be a healthy way to release emotions and can help you feel better.

It's important to allow yourself to feel your emotions and not try to suppress them.

What if I feel like my emotions are too overwhelming?

Answer: It's important to reach out for help if you're feeling overwhelmed. You can talk to a trusted adult or seek professional help from a therapist or counselor. There are also hotlines available for those who need immediate support.

Chapter Five:

YOUR HEIGHT

As you go through puberty, your body will change in many ways, including your height. You may notice that you grow taller quickly or slowly, and you may have questions about when you'll stop growing. In this chapter, we'll explore the changes that happen during this important time in your life and give you tips on how to take care of yourself along the way. Remember, everyone grows at their own pace, so embrace your height and be proud of who you are.

When will I start to get taller?

As a boy going through puberty, you will start to experience growth spurts, which means you will get taller. Most boys start their growth spurt between the ages of 10 and 16, with the average age being 13. During this time, you can expect to grow around 2 to 3 inches per year. However, the timing and rate of your growth can vary, so it's important to remember that everyone develops at their own pace. Genetics also play a significant role in determining your height, so you may end up being taller or shorter than your peers. As you continue to go through puberty, your body will undergo many changes, and your height is just one aspect of this exciting time in your life.

How much will I grow?

The amount that you will grow depends on many factors such as your genetics, nutrition, and overall health. Most boys will experience a growth spurt during puberty, which usually occurs between the ages of 9 and 14. During this time, it is common to grow several inches in a short period. However, growth patterns can vary greatly from person to person. Some boys may stop growing by the time they are 16 years old, while others may continue to grow until they are in their early 20s. Your pediatrician or healthcare provider can help you better understand your individual growth potential based on your family history, growth charts, and other factors.

The amount you will grow during puberty depends on many factors, including your genetics, nutrition, and overall health. On average, boys can grow between 2 and 10 inches (5-25 cm) during puberty, with the greatest growth spurt occurring between ages 12 and 16. However, some boys may continue to grow into their late teens or even early twenties. It's important to remember that everyone grows at their own pace and there is no "right" amount of growth.

Factors that can affect your growth include your diet and nutrition, physical activity levels, and overall health. Ensuring you eat a healthy and balanced diet, getting enough sleep, and staying physically active can all help support healthy growth during puberty. However, if you have concerns about your growth or are not growing as expected, it's important to talk to your healthcare provider. They can help evaluate any underlying medical conditions and provide guidance on healthy lifestyle choices to support your growth and development.

When will I stop growing?

Typically, boys stop growing around the ages of 16-18, but this can vary. Genetics, nutrition, and overall health can all play a role in determining when someone will stop growing. Some boys may continue to grow until their early 20s, while others may stop growing earlier. It's important to remember that everyone grows and develops at their own pace, so it's not necessarily a cause for concern if someone stops growing earlier or later than their peers. Additionally, it's worth noting that while height is largely determined by genetics, there are factors that can influence growth, such as getting enough sleep, eating a healthy diet, and engaging in regular exercise.

Why are so many girls taller than boys in middle school?

It is common for girls to experience growth spurts earlier than boys. Girls typically enter puberty between ages 8 and 13, while boys enter puberty between ages 9 and 14. During puberty, the body produces hormones that stimulate growth and development. In girls, the hormone estrogen is primarily responsible for this growth, while in boys, it is testosterone. Estrogen stimulates the growth of long bones, leading to an increase in height. Boys may experience a delay in their growth spurts as testosterone production takes longer to increase. However, once boys hit their growth spurts, they may continue to grow taller than girls into their late teens. It is important to remember that everyone's growth patterns are different, and there is no set rule for how tall someone will be.

Why do my feet seem so big lately?

During puberty, it's common for different parts of the body to grow at different rates. Feet are one of the body parts that can grow quickly and appear larger than usual. As you grow taller and your body adjusts to support your new height, your feet may also increase in size. Additionally, hormones released during puberty can cause your feet to grow wider and longer. It's also important to make sure that your shoes fit properly and are not contributing to any discomfort or pain. If you're concerned about your foot size or have any discomfort, talk to your doctor or a podiatrist for advice.

What if I'm really unhappy with my height?

Feeling unhappy with your height is not uncommon, but it's important to remember that everyone grows at their own pace and in their own way. It's also important to know that there's not much you can do to change your height, as it's largely determined by genetics.

However, there are a few things you can do to feel more confident and comfortable in your own skin. You can try wearing clothes that fit well and flatter your body shape, as this can help you feel more confident about your appearance. You can also work on your posture, which can make you look taller and more confident.

It's also important to remember that there are many successful and happy people of all heights. Your height does not define who you are as a person or your abilities. Try to focus on your strengths and accomplishments, and don't let your height hold you back from pursuing your goals and dreams. If you're feeling really down about your height, don't be afraid to talk to a trusted friend, family member, or counselor for support and guidance.

I've heard that there is some kind of medicine you can take to get taller. Is this true?

There are some medicines that claim to increase height, but they are generally not effective and can have dangerous side effects. The only proven way to increase height is through a healthy diet and exercise, getting enough sleep, and allowing your body to naturally go through the growth process. It's important to remember that height is just one aspect of physical appearance and does not determine a person's worth or value. It's more important to focus on being healthy and taking care of your body. If you have concerns about your height or any other aspect of your physical appearance, it's always a good idea to talk to a trusted adult or a healthcare provider for guidance and support.

I heard on the news that it's important to build strong bones when you're a kid. Why?

It is important to build strong bones during childhood and adolescence because bones reach their maximum density and strength by the age of 25. Building strong bones at a young age helps prevent bone loss later in life and reduces the risk of developing osteoporosis, a condition where bones become weak and brittle, increasing the risk of fractures. Adequate calcium and vitamin D intake, along with weight-bearing physical activities such as running and jumping, can help build strong bones. It is also important to avoid habits that weaken bones, such as smoking and excessive alcohol consumption.

Chapter Six:

LETS' TALK ABOUT SEX?

As you grow older, you may start to have questions about sex and your body. This chapter will provide you with information on what sex is, how it works, and how to make healthy and safe choices. We will also discuss the changes that occur in your body during puberty and how they relate to sexual development. It is important to have accurate information about sex and your body to make informed decisions and stay healthy.

Why does it seem that boys and girls suddenly don't have as much in common as they used to?

During puberty, boys and girls go through significant physical and emotional changes, which can affect their behavior, interests, and even social circles. While they may have had similar interests and activities in childhood, the differences in hormonal levels and physical development can make it challenging for them to relate to each other. Boys may become more interested in sports, video games, and other traditionally male-dominated activities, while girls may become more interested in fashion, music, and socializing. However, it's important to remember that these are just generalizations, and there is no one-size-fits-all answer. Some boys and girls may continue to have common interests, while others may find new ways to connect and understand each other.

Why does it sometimes feel uncomfortable to be around girls now?

As boys go through puberty, they may start to feel self-conscious or uncomfortable around girls, especially if they are developing crushes or becoming more aware of their own sexuality. This can be a normal part of the process, but it's important to understand that girls are going through similar changes and may feel just as awkward or unsure. It's important to treat girls with respect and kindness, just as you would want to be treated. Remember that everyone is different and goes through puberty at their own pace, so it's important not to judge or make fun of anyone for their development or lack thereof. If you're feeling uncomfortable around girls or have questions about your changing feelings and attractions, talk to a trusted adult or healthcare provider for guidance and support.

What, exactly, is a crush?

A crush is an intense feeling of attraction towards someone. It's a feeling that is often described as a "butterfly in the stomach" or a "racing heart" when you're around the person you have a crush on. You might also find yourself thinking about the person a lot, daydreaming about them, or feeling nervous or anxious around them. Crushes are common during puberty as hormones surge and you begin to develop romantic and sexual feelings. It's important to remember that crushes are a normal part of growing up and can help you understand your own feelings and emotions. However, it's also important to respect the other person's boundaries and feelings, and to not let your crush consume all of your thoughts and actions.

What do I do if I have a crush on a girl?

If you have a crush on a girl, it's completely normal to feel nervous and unsure of what to do. One of the most important things to remember is to respect her and her boundaries. Don't pressure her to like you or do anything she's not comfortable with.

If you want to get to know her better, start by striking up a conversation. Ask her about her interests and hobbies, and share some of your own. If you have common interests, suggest doing something together, like going to see a movie or playing a game.

It's also important to remember that rejection is a possibility. Not everyone will reciprocate your feelings, and that's okay. Don't take it personally and don't give up on finding someone who likes you for who you are.

Ultimately, the most important thing is to be yourself and be confident in who you are. If you're happy with who you are, others will be drawn to that positivity and confidence.

What do I do if a girl has a crush on me?

If a girl has a crush on you, it's important to be kind and respectful to her. You don't have to feel the same way, but it's important not to hurt her feelings or make fun of her. It's okay to let her know that you don't feel the same way, but do it gently and without being mean. Remember that having a crush is a normal part of growing up, and it's not something to be ashamed of. If you do have feelings for her, be honest and let her know, but make sure that you both are ready for a relationship and willing to communicate openly and honestly with each other.

What if I have a crush on another boy?

It's normal to have crushes on people of any gender. If you have a crush on another boy, it's important to remember that your feelings are valid and you shouldn't feel ashamed or guilty about them. However, it's also important to be respectful of other people's boundaries and not make them uncomfortable. If you feel comfortable, you could try talking to a trusted friend or family member about your feelings. You could also consider talking to a counselor or therapist who can provide support and guidance. Ultimately, it's up to you to decide if and when you want to tell the person you have a crush on, but it's important to be respectful and considerate of their feelings.

When are teenagers ready to date?

The age at which teenagers are ready to date can vary depending on the individual. It is important for teenagers to have the maturity and emotional readiness to handle the complexities of relationships. Some teenagers may feel ready to date in their early teens, while others may not feel ready until later. It is also important for parents to be involved in their teenager's dating life and provide guidance and support. Teenagers should have a good understanding of what a healthy relationship looks like and should have open communication with their partner. Ultimately, the decision to date should be made based on individual readiness and comfort level, and with the guidance and support of trusted adults.

While there's no specific age or timeline for when a teenager is "ready" to date, it's important for them to have a good understanding of their own feelings, have good communication skills, and have a sense of respect and boundaries in relationships. Parents can also play a role in guiding their teenagers and helping them navigate the complexities of dating. Ultimately, each teenager should feel comfortable and confident in their decision to start dating and should prioritize their own well-being and safety.

How can I talk to my parents about dating

If you want to talk to your parents about dating, try to choose a good time to have a conversation, when they are not busy or stressed. Be honest about your feelings and let them know why dating is important to you. Be prepared to listen to their perspective and rules. It's also helpful to show responsibility and maturity by being open to their guidance and rules. Remember, your parents want what is best for you, even if you don't always agree with them.

I don't feel ready to date, I don't want to date, I'm too busy with school activities, and my parents won't let me date just yet.

That's okay! It's important to focus on your own personal growth and priorities before pursuing a romantic relationship. You can always revisit the idea of dating in the future when you feel more ready and have more time. Your parents are likely trying to look out for your best interests and keep you safe, so it's important to listen to their guidance and trust their judgement.

Sexual responsibility refers to the actions and decisions individuals make to protect themselves and their partners from sexually transmitted infections (STIs) and unwanted pregnancies. It also involves respecting boundaries and ensuring that any sexual activity is consensual. It is important for young people to learn about sexual responsibility as they enter puberty and begin to explore their sexuality. By being responsible and taking necessary precautions, individuals can avoid negative consequences and maintain healthy relationships. It is also essential to communicate openly and honestly with partners about sexual health and expectations.

Why is it better to wait until I'm older to think about being more sexual with someone?

It is better to wait until you are older to think about being more sexual with someone because sex is a big responsibility that should be taken seriously. Engaging in sexual activities can have emotional, physical and mental consequences that can affect you and your partner's lives. Being sexually active at a young age can also increase the risk of unwanted pregnancies, sexually transmitted infections (STIs), and emotional trauma. It is important to have a clear understanding of your own values and beliefs, and to communicate them with your partner before becoming sexually active. Waiting until you are emotionally and mentally mature, and physically ready can ensure that you make informed decisions and are responsible for your actions. Remember, sex should always be consensual and should never be used as a way to pressure or manipulate someone into doing something they are not comfortable with.

What is sex?

Sex is the act of two people engaging in physical intimacy with each other, usually involving the genitalia. It can lead to reproduction or simply be an expression of love, pleasure, or attraction between two consenting adults. Sex can take many forms and can involve a variety of sexual activities, but it is important to always prioritize safety, respect, and communication with one's partner.

Here are some healthy ways to be close with someone:

- **Communication:** Talk openly and honestly with each other. Share your feelings, concerns, and ideas.
- **Shared interests:** Find activities you both enjoy doing together, such as playing sports, hiking, watching movies, or playing games.
- **Quality time:** Spend time together regularly and make it a priority in your life. This can be as simple as having a meal together or taking a walk.
- **Trust:** Build trust by being reliable and dependable, keeping your promises, and being honest with each other.
- **Respect:** Show respect for each other's feelings, boundaries, and opinions. Avoid being critical or judgmental.
- **Physical touch:** Hugs, holding hands, and other forms of physical touch can help create a sense of closeness and intimacy.
- **Emotional support:** Be there for each other during challenging times, offering encouragement, empathy, and understanding.

Remember, it's important to be mindful of your own and your partner's boundaries and comfort levels. Building a healthy relationship takes time and effort, but it can be a rewarding experience.

What should I do if my friends are pressuring me into having sex?

If your friends are pressuring you into having sex, it's important to remember that you always have the right to say no. It's important to communicate clearly with your friends about your boundaries and let them know that you are not comfortable with their behavior. If they continue to pressure you, it might be necessary to distance yourself from those friends and seek support from trusted adults, such as a parent, teacher, or counselor. Remember, it's never okay for someone to pressure you into doing something you're not comfortable with, especially when it comes to something as personal and intimate as sex. Your body and your decisions are yours alone to make.

What are STDs? How do people get them?

STDs (Sexually Transmitted Diseases) are infections that are transmitted from one person to another through sexual contact, including vaginal, oral, or anal sex. There are many types of STDs, including chlamydia, gonorrhea, herpes, human papillomavirus (HPV), syphilis, and HIV/AIDS.

STDs can be spread through the exchange of bodily fluids, including blood, semen, vaginal fluids, and breast milk. They can also be spread through skin-to-skin contact with infected areas, such as genital warts.

The most effective way to prevent the spread of STDs is to practice safe sex, including the use of condoms, dental dams, and other barrier methods. It's important to get tested regularly for STDs, especially if you are sexually active with multiple partners.

Many STDs can be treated and cured with antibiotics or antiviral medications, but some, like HIV, are incurable and can have serious health consequences if left untreated. It's important to seek medical attention if you think you may have an STD, and to be honest with sexual partners about your sexual health history to prevent the spread of infection.

Here are four common myths about pregnancy for teens:

- You can't get pregnant if you have sex during your period.
- You can't get pregnant if you use the withdrawal method or have sex standing up.
- You can't get pregnant if it's your first time having sex.

- You can't get pregnant if you douche after sex.

It's important for teens to understand that these myths are not true and that pregnancy can occur any time sexual activity takes place. Using reliable forms of contraception, such as condoms or birth control pills, can greatly reduce the risk of unintended pregnancy and sexually transmitted infections (STIs). Additionally, it's important to have open and honest communication with sexual partners and to practice safe sex. Teens should also be aware of the potential emotional, physical, and financial consequences of becoming pregnant at a young age, and should consider seeking support and guidance from trusted adults, healthcare providers, or community resources.

Condoms have been in use for at least 400 years. In ancient times, they were made from materials like animal bladders, linen, and even tortoise shells.

Behaviors that are never okay

- **Sexual assault** is any unwanted sexual contact, such as touching or groping. It is a crime, and no one has the right to touch or have sexual contact with someone without their consent.
- **Sexual harassment** is unwanted or unwelcome sexual advances, comments, or gestures. It can happen at school, work, or in any social setting. It is important to speak up and report any instances of sexual harassment.

- **Sexual abuse or molestation** is any sexual activity that occurs without the other person's consent. This can include inappropriate touching, exposing oneself, or forcing someone to engage in sexual activity. It is important to seek help and support if you have experienced sexual abuse or molestation.

It is never okay for someone to touch or engage in sexual activity with you without your consent. It is important to know your rights and boundaries, and to speak up if you feel uncomfortable or unsafe in any situation. There are resources and support available to help you if you have experienced any form of sexual assault, harassment, or abuse.

Chapter Seven:

EXERCISING AND BUILDING A HEALTHY WEIGHT

Exercising and maintaining a healthy weight are essential for overall health and well-being. During puberty, your body undergoes significant changes, and exercise can help you manage these changes while also building a strong foundation for a healthy future. In this chapter, we will explore the benefits of exercise, including its impact on your physical health, mental well-being, and self-esteem. We will also discuss how to develop an exercise plan that works for you, as well as ways to stay motivated and make exercise a regular part of your daily routine. With the right mindset and approach, you can build a healthy weight and enjoy the many benefits of an active lifestyle.

Why do I need to pay attention to what I eat?

Eating healthy is crucial for your growth and development during puberty. Consuming a balanced diet can help you build muscle, maintain a healthy weight, and provide you with the nutrients your body needs to function properly. Paying attention to what you eat can also help you avoid unwanted weight gain or loss. Be sure to include a variety of food groups in your meals, such as lean proteins, whole grains, fruits, and vegetables. Avoid consuming too much processed or junk food, as they are typically high in calories and low in nutrients. Additionally, limit your intake of sugary drinks and snacks, as they can contribute to tooth decay and weight gain. Remember to also stay hydrated by drinking plenty of water throughout the day. Making healthy food choices now can set you up for a lifetime of good eating habits and better health overall.

How often do I need to eat?

You should aim to eat three regular meals a day with snacks in between if you are still hungry. Eating at regular intervals helps to keep your metabolism steady and prevents overeating. Skipping meals can lead to overeating later on and can also affect your energy levels and concentration. It's important to listen to your body's hunger and fullness signals to determine how much and when to eat. If you have specific dietary needs or health concerns, you may need to eat more frequently or follow a specific meal plan recommended by a healthcare professional.

Do you ever have this happen to you?

- *If you don't eat breakfast, you get a headache in the*
- *middle of the morning.*
- *You do poorly on a test.*
- *You fall asleep in class.*
- *You're having trouble paying attention to the teacher.*

The frequency at which you eat is important to maintain a healthy metabolism and energy levels throughout the day. It's generally recommended to eat three main meals per day (breakfast, lunch, and dinner) with healthy snacks in between if needed. Some people may also benefit from eating smaller, more frequent meals throughout the day, such as five or six meals instead of three. This approach may help regulate blood sugar levels and prevent overeating.

Ultimately, the frequency at which you eat should be determined by your own individual needs and preferences. It's important to listen to your body's hunger cues and eat when you're hungry, rather than restricting yourself or forcing yourself to eat when you're not hungry. Consistency is key, so aim to eat meals and snacks around the same time each day to establish a healthy routine.

What kind of food should I eat?

Food Groups	Examples
Fruits	Bananas, apples, oranges, berries, melons
Vegetables	Broccoli, spinach, carrots, peppers, sweet potatoes
Protein	Chicken, fish, lean beef, beans, tofu
Whole Grains	Brown rice, whole wheat bread, quinoa, oatmeal, popcorn
Diary	Mil, cheese, yogurt, cottage cheese
Healthy Fats	Avocado, nuts, seeds, olive oil, fatty fish

It's important to have a balanced and varied diet that includes all food groups in appropriate portions. It's also important to limit intake of processed and sugary foods, and to stay hydrated by drinking plenty of water. Consult with a doctor or registered dietitian for personalized nutrition advice.

How can I eat well at school?

Eating well at school is important for maintaining a healthy lifestyle. Here are some tips on how to eat well at school:

- **Pack your lunch:** By packing your lunch, you have control over what you eat. Include foods from all food groups, such as fruits, vegetables, whole grains, lean proteins, and low-fat dairy products.

- **Choose wisely from the cafeteria:** If you eat from the school cafeteria, choose foods that are lower in fat, sugar, and sodium. Look for whole grain options, fresh fruits and vegetables, and lean protein sources.

- **Don't skip breakfast:** Eating breakfast gives you energy for the day ahead. Choose a balanced breakfast that includes whole grains, fruits or vegetables, and lean proteins.
- **Bring healthy snacks:** Instead of reaching for chips or candy from the vending machine, bring healthy snacks from home, such as fresh fruit, baby carrots, or low-fat yogurt.
- **Drink plenty of water:** Staying hydrated is important for your overall health. Carry a refillable water bottle and drink water throughout the day.
- Remember, eating well at school is an important part of maintaining a healthy lifestyle.

What if I want to try out a different diet, like vegetarian?

If you're interested in trying out a different diet, such as a vegetarian one, it's important to do your research first. While a vegetarian diet can be a healthy and nutritious choice, it's important to make sure you're getting all the necessary nutrients your body needs.

Start by learning more about vegetarianism and what types of foods you can eat. Vegetarian diets typically include plenty of fruits, vegetables, whole grains, legumes, nuts, and seeds. It's important to pay attention to getting enough protein, calcium, iron, and vitamin B12, which are nutrients that can be more challenging to get enough of on a vegetarian diet.

If you're interested in trying a vegetarian diet, consider talking to a nutritionist or registered dietitian who can help you develop a meal plan that meets your nutritional needs. You can also do some research and find resources online, such as vegetarian cookbooks or websites, that can provide ideas and inspiration for meals.

It's important to listen to your body and make sure you're feeling well and getting enough energy to support your activities. Remember that a healthy diet includes a variety of foods from all food groups, and it's okay to indulge in treats occasionally. Make sure to enjoy your food and nourish your body in a way that works for you.

Is exercise important?

Yes, exercise is very important for maintaining good physical and mental health. It can help improve cardiovascular health, build strength and endurance, boost mood, reduce stress and anxiety, and prevent chronic diseases. Regular exercise can also help maintain a healthy weight, improve sleep quality, and increase overall energy levels.

How do I avoid sports injuries?

Sports injuries are common among athletes, but there are ways to prevent them. First, it's essential to warm up and stretch properly before engaging in any physical activity. This helps to prepare the body for the demands of the sport and reduce the risk of injury. Second, it's important to wear appropriate gear and equipment, such as helmets, pads, and shoes that fit well and provide proper support. Third, athletes should listen to their bodies and take breaks when they're feeling fatigued or in pain. Overuse injuries can occur when the body is pushed too hard and doesn't have time to recover. Fourth, athletes should cross-train to build strength and flexibility in all areas of the body, not just the ones used in their sport. This can help prevent imbalances and overuse injuries. Finally, athletes should follow a healthy diet and get enough rest and recovery time. This helps to keep the body strong and able to handle the demands of training and competition. By following these guidelines, athletes can reduce their risk of sports injuries and stay healthy and strong.

My parents keep bugging me about how much time I spend playing video games. What's the big deal?

Your parents may be concerned about the amount of time you spend playing games because it can interfere with your daily activities and affect your physical and mental health. Playing games for an extended period can lead to physical problems, such as eyestrain, neck and back pain, and carpal tunnel syndrome. It can also contribute to an unhealthy lifestyle if it means you are not getting enough exercise, eating poorly, or not getting enough sleep. In addition, excessive gaming can negatively affect your mental health, causing addiction, social isolation, and depression.

Your parents may also be worried about the content of the games you are playing. Some games may have violent or sexual content that is not appropriate for your age group. Exposure to these themes can have a negative impact on your emotional and psychological well-being, and your parents may be concerned about your exposure to them.

It's essential to communicate with your parents about your gaming habits and assure them that you are still able to maintain your responsibilities and other activities. Consider setting limits on your gaming time and balance it with other activities, such as exercise and socializing. Additionally, you can research and choose age-appropriate games that are educational and challenging.

Is it okay for kids my age to lift weights?

It depends on a few factors. Generally, lifting weights is safe for teenagers as long as they use proper technique, start with light weights and gradually increase, and have adult supervision or guidance from a certified trainer. It's also important to make sure you're getting enough rest and not overtraining. However, if you have certain medical conditions or injuries, you may need to avoid or modify certain exercises. It's always a good idea to check with a doctor before starting a new exercise program, especially if you have any concerns or questions.

Don't Overdo It!

Sure, it's important to maintain a healthy exercise routine, but it's equally important not to overdo it. Over-exercising can lead to injuries and exhaustion, and can also interfere with other important activities such as schoolwork, socializing, and relaxation. It's important to listen to your body and give it time to rest and recover. Consult with a doctor or trainer to ensure that your exercise routine is safe and effective. Remember, balance is key!

What changes can I expect to see in my body?

It's important to have realistic expectations for your body and to focus on being healthy rather than achieving a specific appearance. Eating a balanced diet and exercising regularly can help you build strength and improve your overall fitness. Resistance training, such as weightlifting, can help build muscle mass, while cardio exercises like running or biking can help burn fat. It's important to work with a trainer or coach to develop a safe and effective exercise plan. Remember to listen to your body and avoid pushing yourself too hard, as over-exercising can lead to injuries and burnout. Finally, remember that everybody is different and it's okay to embrace your unique shape and size.

What am I supposed to weigh?

Your ideal weight depends on your age, height, body composition, and overall health. It's best to consult a healthcare professional to determine what weight is appropriate for you.

What do I do if I think I'm overweight?

If you are concerned that you may be overweight, it is important to talk to your doctor or a qualified healthcare professional. They can help you assess your current weight, body mass index (BMI), and overall health to determine if you are truly overweight or if there may be underlying health issues that need to be addressed.

If you are indeed overweight, there are a few things you can do to improve your health and lose weight in a healthy way. These include:

- **Eating a balanced diet:** focus on eating whole, unprocessed foods like fruits, vegetables, lean proteins, and whole grains, and limit your intake of processed and high-fat foods.
- **Engaging in regular physical activity:** aim for at least 30 minutes of moderate exercise most days of the week, and try to find activities that you enjoy.
- **Seeking support:** consider working with a registered dietitian, a personal trainer, or a support group to help you stay on track and achieve your goals.

Remember, weight loss should always be done in a healthy and sustainable way. Quick-fix diets or extreme exercise routines can be harmful to your health and are unlikely to lead to long-term success.

What if I'm unhappy with my body?

It's important to remember that everyone's body is different and there is no one "perfect" body. However, if you are feeling unhappy with your body, there are some things you can do.

Firstly, try to focus on making healthy choices rather than obsessing over your appearance. This means eating nutritious foods, getting regular exercise, and practicing good self-care habits.

It's also important to surround yourself with positive influences, such as friends and family members who support and encourage you.

If your negative body image is affecting your mental health, consider speaking to a counselor or therapist who can help you work through your feelings and develop a more positive self-image.

Remember, it's not always easy to love your body, but with time and practice, you can learn to appreciate and care for the body you have.

What are anabolic steroids?

Anabolic steroids are synthetic versions of the male hormone testosterone. They are often used illegally to increase muscle mass and improve athletic performance. Anabolic steroids are available in various forms, including pills, injections, gels, and creams. They are typically used in cycles, with periods of use followed by periods of abstinence.

Anabolic steroids can have serious and potentially life-threatening side effects, including liver damage, kidney damage, heart disease, high blood pressure, and stroke. They can also cause a number of other health problems, including acne, hair loss, infertility, and mood swings.

Anabolic steroid use is illegal without a prescription, and it is banned by most professional sports organizations. In addition to the health risks associated with anabolic steroid use, there are also legal consequences. Possession or sale of anabolic steroids can result in fines, jail time, and other penalties.

It is important to remember that there are no shortcuts to building a healthy, strong body. Regular exercise, a balanced diet, and adequate rest are essential for achieving and maintaining a healthy weight and a fit physique. If you are considering using anabolic steroids or other performance-enhancing drugs, it is important to talk to a healthcare professional about the risks and potential consequences.

Chapter Eight:

YOUR REPRODUCTIVE SYSTEM

This chapter will explore the anatomy and function of the male and female reproductive systems. It will cover everything from the internal organs to external genitalia, as well as the processes involved in reproduction. Understanding your reproductive system is important for overall health and wellbeing, as well as making informed decisions about sexual activity and family planning. We will also cover common issues that can occur with the reproductive system, such as infections and infertility. Whether you are male or female, understanding your reproductive system is an important part of growing up and taking control of your health. So, let's dive in and explore the fascinating world of your reproductive system.

What are the testicles and the scrotum, actually?

The testicles and scrotum are part of the male reproductive system. The testicles, also known as testes, are two small oval-shaped organs that produce sperm and the hormone testosterone. They are located inside the scrotum, a sac of skin that hangs outside the body between the legs. The scrotum helps regulate the temperature of the testicles, which is important for sperm production. During puberty, the testicles and scrotum begin to develop and grow, leading to changes in the male body. Understanding the anatomy and function of the testicles and scrotum is important for overall reproductive and sexual health in males.

Testosterone is the most important male sex hormone, but it's also present in females, just at lower levels.

The testicles are two oval-shaped glands located in the scrotum that produce and store sperm and testosterone. The scrotum is a sac of skin that hangs behind the penis and contains the testicles. The scrotum helps regulate the temperature of the testicles to keep them slightly cooler than body temperature, which is necessary for sperm production. During puberty, the testicles begin to grow and produce more testosterone, leading to the development of male secondary sexual characteristics, such as a deeper voice, facial hair, and muscle growth. It's important to regularly check the testicles for any unusual lumps or swelling, which could be a sign of a medical condition.

What is the penis made of?

The penis is made of three main parts: the root, shaft, and glans. It also contains blood vessels, nerves, and urethra.

What reproductive organs are inside my body, and what do they do?

There are several internal reproductive organs in the male body that play important roles in the production and delivery of sperm. The testicles are responsible for producing and storing sperm, which are carried to the prostate gland through a series of ducts known as the epididymis. The prostate gland, along with the seminal vesicles and bulbourethral glands, produce semen, which is the fluid that carries the sperm during ejaculation. The vas deferens is the tube that carries the sperm from the epididymis to the urethra, where it is expelled during ejaculation. These organs work together to ensure that the sperm is produced, stored, and delivered effectively for reproduction.

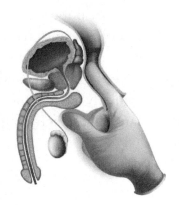

Why does my penis get hard sometimes?

An erection happens when the spongy tissue in the penis fills up with blood, causing it to become firm and stand away from the body. Erections can happen spontaneously or in response to sexual stimulation. Hormones, nerve impulses, and psychological factors can all contribute to the process. While it is a normal physiological response, it is important to remember to always respect other people's boundaries and consent when it comes to sexual activities.

My penis curves to one side. Is this normal?

Penis curvature is common and usually not a cause for concern. It can happen naturally or due to scar tissue buildup. In most cases, a slight curve is harmless and doesn't affect sexual function. However, if the curvature is severe or causes pain during erection, it may be a condition called Peyronie's disease and should be evaluated by a healthcare provider.

How will my genitals change as I get older?

As you grow older, your genitals will undergo a number of changes. During puberty, you will start to produce more hormones that will trigger the growth and development of your genitals. Your testicles will become larger and will start to produce sperm. Your penis will also grow in length and girth, and you will begin to experience spontaneous erections and ejaculation.

It's important to remember that everyone's body is different and will undergo changes at its own pace. If you have concerns about the changes you are experiencing or have questions about your sexual health, it's important to talk to a trusted healthcare provider who can provide guidance and support.

I worry that my penis is too small. How do I know if I'm normal?

It's common to worry about penis size during adolescence. Most boys have a penis that falls within the average range of 2.5 to 4 inches when flaccid and 4.5 to 7 inches when erect. If you're concerned, talk to a trusted adult or healthcare provider who can provide more information and reassurance. Remember, penis size doesn't determine sexual pleasure or satisfaction.

What's the difference between a circumcised penis and an uncircumcised one?

Circumcision is a surgical procedure where the foreskin, the skin covering the head of the penis, is removed. An uncircumcised penis has a foreskin that covers the head of the penis. Circumcised and uncircumcised penises differ in appearance and sensitivity, but both can be normal and healthy. Some people choose to have their children circumcised for religious or cultural reasons, while others choose not to because they believe it is unnecessary. There are also medical reasons to circumcise, such as a tight foreskin that makes it difficult to keep the penis clean, or repeated infections of the foreskin.

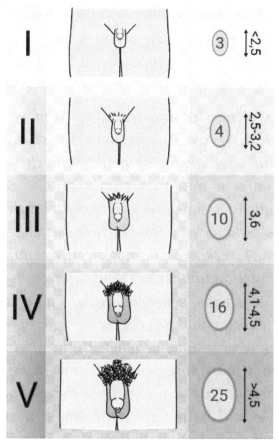

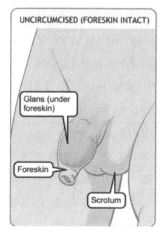

UNCIRCUMCISED (FORESKIN INTACT)

Glans (under foreskin)

Foreskin

Scrotum

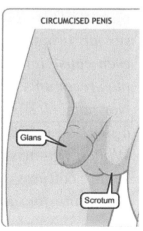

CIRCUMCISED PENIS

Glans

Scrotum

What should I know if I'm not circumcised?

If you are not circumcised, it means that the foreskin, a loose fold of skin that covers the head of the penis, is still intact. Here are some things to keep in mind:

- *Hygiene: It's important to keep your penis clean to avoid infection. You should gently pull back the foreskin and clean the area with soap and water.*
- *Smegma: Smegma is a natural lubricant that is produced by the body. It can collect under the foreskin, and if not cleaned regularly, can cause an unpleasant smell or even infection.*
- *Sex: During sex, the foreskin can retract, and this can add to the sensation of pleasure. However, some people with foreskin may find that it is more sensitive, and they may need to take care during sex to avoid discomfort.*
- *Medical issues: In some cases, the foreskin may be too tight, making it difficult to retract. This can lead to discomfort during sex or urination, and in severe cases, can even cause infection. In such cases, a doctor may recommend circumcision as a solution.*
- *Normalcy: It's important to know that having a foreskin is completely normal and healthy. While circumcision is a common practice in some cultures and religions, it is not necessary for good health. It's a personal*

choice that should be made by the individual or their parents based on their own beliefs and medical needs.

How should I take care of an uncircumcised penis?

If you are uncircumcised, it is important to keep your penis clean to prevent infections. Gently pull back the foreskin and wash the area with warm water daily, using only mild soap. Avoid using harsh soaps or scrubbing too hard as it can irritate the sensitive skin. Rinse thoroughly and pat dry with a clean towel. It is also important to keep the area dry, as moisture can cause infections. If you notice any redness, swelling, or discharge, see a healthcare provider.

Why do I need to worry about cancer in a testicle? I'm only a teenager.

Testicular cancer is rare in teenagers, but it can occur. It is important to know the symptoms and risks associated with this disease. Testicular cancer usually occurs in men aged 15 to 35. The most common symptom is a lump or swelling in one of the testicles. Other symptoms include pain or discomfort in the testicle or scrotum, a feeling of heaviness in the scrotum, and back pain.

Testicular cancer can be aggressive and spread to other parts of the body if not caught early. The good news is that it is one of the most treatable forms of cancer with a high survival rate if caught early. It is important to perform a self-examination of the testicles regularly to check for any lumps, swelling or changes in size. If you notice any of these symptoms, you should see a doctor immediately.

It is also important to know that testicular cancer is more common in men who have had an undescended testicle at birth or have a family history of the disease. It is recommended that boys with an undescended testicle have surgery to correct the condition before puberty to reduce the risk of testicular cancer later in life.

I have some light-colored bumps around the head of my penis. Is something wrong?

It is possible that the bumps you are seeing are a normal part of your anatomy, such as Fordyce spots or pearly penile papules. However, it is important to have any changes in the appearance of your genital area checked by a doctor, as these bumps could also be a sign of an infection or a sexually transmitted disease. It is important to be honest with your doctor about your sexual history, as this can help with diagnosis and treatment. Don't be embarrassed to seek medical help, as many genital conditions are common and easily treatable with early intervention.

I felt something soft and bumpy in my scrotum. What could it be?

Feeling something soft and bumpy in your scrotum can be concerning, but it's important to stay calm and get it checked out by a doctor. It could be a number of things, such as a cyst, a varicocele, or even a testicular tumor. A cyst is a fluid-filled sac that can develop anywhere in the body, including the scrotum. A varicocele is a swelling of the veins that drain the testicle, and it is more common on the left side. A testicular tumor is a growth that can be benign or cancerous. It's important to get any lumps or bumps checked out by a doctor, who can perform a physical exam and order imaging tests, such as an ultrasound, if necessary. Remember, early detection is key for successful treatment.

My doctor says I have undescended testicles. What does that mean?

Undescended testicles, also known as cryptorchidism, is a condition where one or both testicles fail to move from the abdomen to the scrotum during fetal development. It is a common condition in newborns and typically resolves on its own within a few months. However, if the testicles do not descend on their own, treatment may be necessary. Undescended testicles can increase the risk of infertility, testicular cancer, and other complications if left untreated. Treatment options may include hormone therapy or surgery to bring the testicles into the scrotum. If you have been diagnosed with undescended testicles, it is important to discuss the best course of treatment with your doctor.

I have lumps under my nipples and they sometimes feel sore. What's happening? Could I be growing breasts?

The lumps you are feeling under your nipples are likely due to a condition called gynecomastia, which is the enlargement of breast tissue in males. This condition is not uncommon during puberty and is caused by hormonal changes that occur during this time. It is usually not a serious medical concern, but it can cause some discomfort or embarrassment. In most cases, the condition resolves on its own within a few months to a few years. However, in some cases, medical treatment may be necessary, such as hormone therapy or surgery, especially if the condition persists or causes significant psychological distress. If you are concerned about gynecomastia or any other changes in your body, it is best to speak with a healthcare provider.

Chapter Nine:

YOUR HAIR, SKIN AND TEETH

As a teenager, your body is going through many changes, including changes to your skin, teeth, and hair. During puberty, your skin may become oily or dry, you may experience more acne, and hair may start to grow in new places. Your teeth may also shift as your jaw grows, and you may need to start taking care of your teeth differently. Meanwhile, your hair may become oilier or drier, and you may experience hair growth in new places, including your face, chest, and armpits. In this chapter, we'll explore these changes in more detail, and offer tips on how to keep your skin, teeth, and hair healthy and looking great.

Why do I have pimples all of a sudden?

As you go through puberty, hormonal changes cause your body to produce more sebum, an oily substance that helps keep your skin hydrated. However, too much sebum can clog your pores, leading to the development of pimples. This is especially true in areas like your face, chest, and back, where sebaceous glands are more active. Additionally, bacteria that live on your skin can cause inflammation and infection in clogged pores, making pimples worse. While pimples can be a nuisance, they're a common part of puberty and usually go away on their own as your hormones stabilize. There are things you can do to manage your acne, such as keeping your skin clean and avoiding oily or greasy products. In severe cases, a dermatologist may prescribe medication to help clear up your skin.

Can stress affect my skin?

Yes, stress can affect your skin. When you are stressed, your body produces hormones that can increase oil production and cause inflammation, leading to acne breakouts or other skin problems. Stress can also make existing skin conditions worse.

What are blackheads and whiteheads?

Blackheads and whiteheads are both types of acne that occur when hair follicles become clogged with oil and dead skin cells. Blackheads are open comedones that appear as small, dark bumps on the skin's surface. The dark color is caused by the accumulation of oil and dead skin cells, which react with the air and turn dark. Whiteheads, on the other hand, are closed comedones that appear as small, white or skin-colored bumps on the skin. They are formed when a hair follicle becomes clogged but remains closed, preventing the oil and dead skin cells from reacting with the air. Both blackheads and whiteheads are a common problem during puberty, but can also occur at any age.

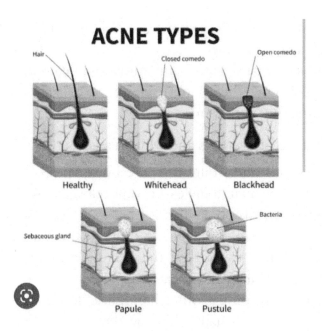

What is acne?

Acne is a common skin condition that occurs when hair follicles become clogged with oil and dead skin cells. This can result in the formation of blackheads, whiteheads, pimples, and cysts. Acne can occur on the face, neck, chest, back, and shoulders. It is most commonly associated with the teenage years, but can occur at any age. Acne can be caused by a variety of factors including hormones, genetics, stress, and certain medications. Proper skin care, including gentle cleansing and moisturizing, can help prevent and reduce the severity of acne. In some cases, medical treatment such as topical or oral medications may be necessary to effectively manage acne.

How do I get rid of my pimples?

Pimples are a common problem for teenagers going through puberty, but they can be frustrating and embarrassing. While there is no single, foolproof cure for pimples, there are several things you can do to help prevent them and reduce their severity:

- ***Keep your face clean:*** *Wash your face twice a day with a gentle cleanser, and avoid scrubbing too hard, as this can irritate your skin.*
- ***Don't touch your face:*** *Your hands carry bacteria, so avoid touching your face to prevent the spread of germs.*
- ***Use oil-free products:*** *Choose products that are oil-free and noncomedogenic, which means they won't clog your pores.*
- ***Eat a healthy diet:*** *A balanced diet that includes plenty of fruits and vegetables can help keep your skin healthy.*
- ***Exercise regularly:*** *Exercise can help reduce stress, which can contribute to acne.*
- ***Avoid picking or squeezing pimples****: This can lead to scarring and can make the problem worse.*
- ***Use acne-fighting products:*** *Over-the-counter acne medications containing benzoyl peroxide or salicylic acid can help reduce pimples.*

- ***Consider seeing a dermatologist:*** *If your acne is severe or not responding to treatment, a dermatologist can help you develop a treatment plan.*

It's important to remember that getting rid of pimples takes time and patience. Don't get discouraged if your acne doesn't clear up overnight, and be consistent with your skincare routine. If you're feeling self-conscious about your acne, remember that it's a common problem, and there's no need to be ashamed. With the right care, your skin will clear up over time.

What other kinds of skin conditions could I get?

There are many other skin conditions that can develop during puberty. Here are a few examples:

- **Eczema:** a chronic condition where the skin becomes red, itchy, and scaly. It can be triggered by allergens, stress, and other factors.

- **Psoriasis:** an autoimmune condition that causes patches of thick, scaly skin. It is often triggered by stress, infections, and other factors.
- **Rosacea:** a chronic condition that causes redness, pimples, and visible blood vessels on the face. It can be triggered by sun exposure, stress, and other factors.
- **Hives:** raised, red, itchy bumps on the skin that can be triggered by allergens, stress, and other factors.
- **Warts:** small, rough growths on the skin that are caused by a viral infection. They can appear on the hands, feet, and genitals.
- **Athlete's foot:** a fungal infection that causes itching, burning, and cracking of the skin on the feet. It can be prevented by keeping feet clean and dry, and wearing clean socks and shoes.
- **Ringworm:** a fungal infection that causes a circular rash on the skin. It can be prevented by avoiding skin-to-skin contact with infected individuals and keeping skin clean and dry.

It's important to remember that many skin conditions are treatable with over-the-counter or prescription medications, and that seeking medical advice is always a good idea if you're experiencing any skin concerns. Additionally, maintaining good hygiene and healthy habits, such as regular exercise and a balanced diet, can help keep your skin in good condition.

What else do I need to do to take care of my skin?

Taking care of your skin involves more than just treating acne and preventing sunburn. Other aspects of skin care include keeping it clean by washing with a gentle cleanser, avoiding harsh scrubs that can damage the skin, using a moisturizer to prevent dryness, and avoiding picking or squeezing pimples or other blemishes. It's also important to protect your skin from the sun by using sunscreen, wearing protective clothing, and avoiding prolonged exposure during peak hours. Eating a healthy diet, drinking plenty of water, and getting enough sleep can also contribute to healthy skin. If you notice any changes in your skin, such as new moles or unusual rashes, it's important to see a doctor for evaluation.

My parents are always telling me not to spend so much time in the sun and they always make me wear sunscreen. What's the big deal?

Exposure to sunlight can be harmful because it emits ultraviolet (UV) radiation, which can damage your skin and increase your risk of developing skin cancer. Sunburns, premature aging, and eye damage are also potential risks of excessive sun exposure. Wearing sunscreen with a high sun protection factor (SPF) can help protect your skin from harmful UV rays. It's important to use sunscreen every day, even on cloudy or overcast days, and to reapply it regularly, especially if you're swimming or sweating. It's also a good idea to wear protective clothing, such as hats and long-sleeved shirts, and to seek shade during peak sun hours, which are typically from 10 a.m. to 4 p.m. By taking these precautions, you can help keep your skin healthy and reduce your risk of developing skin problems later in life.

What is Jock Itch?

Jock itch, also known as tinea cruris, is a fungal infection that affects the skin of the groin area, inner thighs, and buttocks. It is most common in boys and men who sweat a lot, but it can affect anyone. The infection is caused by a type of fungus that thrives in warm, moist environments. Symptoms include redness, itching, and burning in the affected area, as well as a rash that may spread to the buttocks and inner thighs. Jock itch can be treated with over-the-counter antifungal creams or powders, but in some cases, prescription-strength medications may be necessary. Good hygiene practices, such as keeping the area clean and dry, wearing clean underwear, and avoiding tight-fitting clothing, can also help prevent jock itch from developing.

Lately, my feet sometimes smell. What can I do?

Foot odor is a common issue, especially in puberty. It is caused by sweat and bacteria. To reduce foot odor, it is important to keep your feet clean and dry. This means washing your feet daily with soap and water, and thoroughly drying them afterward. Wear clean socks made of breathable materials like cotton or wool, and change them every day. Avoid wearing shoes without socks, and alternate shoes so they have a chance to air out and dry. You can also use antifungal foot powder or spray, which will help to kill bacteria and reduce odor. If these measures do not work, you may need to see a doctor, as persistent foot odor can be a sign of an underlying medical condition such as a fungal infection.

Are piercings and tattoos safe?

Piercing and tattoos can be safe if proper precautions are taken. When getting a tattoo or piercing, it's important to ensure that the artist is licensed and follows proper hygiene practices, such as using sterilized needles and equipment. The artist should also use fresh ink and dispose of used materials properly.

It's also important to take proper care of the tattoo or piercing after it's done. This means keeping the area clean and following any aftercare instructions provided by the artist. If you notice any signs of infection, such as redness, swelling, or discharge, it's important to seek medical attention immediately.

It's also important to consider the potential risks and drawbacks before getting a tattoo or piercing. For example, some people may be allergic to certain types of ink or metals used in piercings, which can cause serious health problems. Additionally, tattoos and piercings can make it harder to get certain types of medical imaging, such as MRIs.

In general, it's a good idea to do your research and make an informed decision before getting a tattoo or piercing. This includes choosing a reputable artist and considering the potential risks and benefits.

Why do I have to brush and floss my teeth every day?

You need to brush and floss your teeth every day to remove the plaque, a sticky film of bacteria that forms on your teeth. Plaque can build up and cause cavities (tooth decay) and gum disease. Brushing your teeth twice a day, flossing at least once a day, and using mouthwash can help to prevent these problems. Additionally, it can also help to keep your breath fresh and your teeth looking clean and white. It's important to use a toothbrush with soft bristles and toothpaste that contains fluoride, which helps to strengthen tooth enamel and fight tooth decay. Regular visits to the dentist for cleanings and checkups are also essential to maintaining good oral health. By following these habits, you can keep your teeth and gums healthy and prevent dental problems in the future.

When will I start to grow underarm hair?

On average, boys begin to grow underarm hair between the ages of 9 and 14, usually starting around age 11. However, the timing can vary from person to person.

Does having hair under my arms have anything to do with using deodorant?

Yes, having hair under your arms can impact the effectiveness of deodorant. Sweat is odorless, but the bacteria that live on your skin can produce an odor when they break down sweat. Armpit hair can trap sweat and bacteria, which can lead to a stronger odor. This is why many people choose to shave or trim their underarm hair. However, it is important to note that shaving can also irritate the skin, so it is important to be gentle and use a clean razor. Additionally, some people choose to use natural deodorants, which may be less effective but are often less irritating to the skin. Ultimately, it is important to find a hygiene routine that works for you and keeps you feeling fresh and clean.

What is pubic hair?

Pubic hair refers to the hair that grows in the pubic area between the belly button and the genitals. During puberty, hormonal changes cause hair to grow in this area, typically starting with a small amount of light hair and eventually becoming thicker, darker, and coarser. Pubic hair serves several functions, including providing a cushioning effect during sex, trapping bacteria and other debris to prevent infection, and helping to regulate body temperature. While pubic hair is a normal and healthy part of development, some people choose to remove or groom their pubic hair for personal or cultural reasons.

The five stages of pubic hair development are:

- ✓ **Stage 1:** No pubic hair is present, only fine vellus hair.
- ✓ **Stage 2:** Sparse growth of long, downy hair, usually straight or only slightly curled.
- ✓ **Stage 3:** Hair becomes darker, curlier, and spreads across the pubic area.
- ✓ **Stage 4:** Hair is thicker and coarser, and spreads to the thighs but not up to the navel.
- ✓ **Stage 5:** Hair is adult-like, covering the entire pubic area and spreading to the thighs and up the abdomen towards the navel.

When will I start to grow pubic hair?

The age at which boys start to grow pubic hair varies widely, but it usually begins sometime between ages 9 and 15. The first sign of pubic hair growth is usually a few soft hairs that appear on the scrotum or at the base of the penis. Over time, the hair will become darker and thicker, and it will spread to the pubic area and upper thighs. The amount and thickness of pubic hair that a boy will develop is largely determined by genetics, and it can take several years for it to fully grow in. It's important to remember that everyone develops at their own pace, and there is no "right" or "wrong" time to start growing pubic hair.

When will I start to grow facial hair?

Boys typically begin to grow facial hair between the ages of 14 and 16, but it can happen as early as age 11 or as late as age 21. The exact timing of facial hair growth varies from person to person and is largely determined by genetics and hormones.

Where will I first notice facial hair

Facial hair typically begins to appear during puberty, when hormone production increases in the body. The first place you might notice facial hair is on your upper lip in the form of a thin, light-colored mustache. This can appear as early as age 11, but for some boys, it may not come in until later.

After the mustache, you may start to notice hair growing on your chin and around your jawline. This hair may initially be sparse and patchy, but it will become thicker and more uniform over time. Hair may also appear on your cheeks, sideburns, and neck.

The pattern of facial hair growth can vary widely between individuals. Some boys may have a full beard by their mid-teens, while others may not have a significant amount of facial hair until their early twenties or later. The color and texture of facial hair can also differ between individuals.

It's important to note that the growth of facial hair is largely determined by genetics. While there are things you can do to encourage healthy hair growth, such as maintaining good nutrition and keeping your skin clean and moisturized, the amount and pattern of facial hair you develop is largely outside of your control.

How do I shave?

To shave, you'll need a razor, shaving cream, and water. First, wet your face with warm water to soften the hair. Then, apply shaving cream and use a razor to shave in the direction of hair growth. Rinse your face with cool water and apply aftershave or moisturizer.

There are two basic types of razors: electric and manual. Electric razors use a motor to move the blades, while manual razors require shaving cream and use the hand to move the razor across the skin. Both types have their own advantages and disadvantages, and it's important to choose the one that suits your needs and preferences.

Here are 5 basic steps for shaving with a disposable razor:

✓ **Wet your face:** First, wash your face with warm water or take a shower to soften your facial hair and open your pores. This will help the razor to glide more smoothly over your skin.

✓ **Apply shaving cream or gel:** Apply a thin layer of shaving cream or gel to the areas you want to shave. This will help to lubricate your skin and protect it from irritation.

✓ **Shave:** Hold the razor at a 30-degree angle and shave in the direction of hair growth. Be gentle and take short strokes to avoid nicks and cuts.

✓ **Rinse the razor frequently:** Rinse the razor under warm water after every few strokes to remove hair and shaving cream. This will help to prevent the razor from getting clogged and ensure a close shave.

✓ **Rinse your face and apply aftershave:** After you have finished shaving, rinse your face with cool water and pat it dry with a clean towel. Then, apply an aftershave lotion or balm to soothe and moisturize your skin.

Make sure to prepare your skin beforehand with warm water and shaving cream, use a sharp razor, shave in the direction of hair growth, rinse your blade often, and moisturize your skin afterwards to prevent irritation.

How do you shave with an electric razor?
The three fundamentals of using an electric razor are:

- **Clean and dry skin:** It is important to have a clean and dry face before using an electric razor to ensure a smoother and closer shave.

- **Proper technique:** Unlike traditional razors, an electric razor should be moved in a circular or back-and-forth motion against the grain of the hair to achieve the best results.

- **Regular maintenance:** Keeping the electric razor clean and maintained is crucial for its longevity and performance. Regularly replacing the blades and cleaning the razor can prevent irritation and ensure a close, comfortable shave.

What should I do if I develop a skin problem from shaving?

If you develop a skin problem from shaving, it's important to take care of the affected area. First, stop shaving until the skin has healed completely. Use warm water and gentle soap to clean the area and pat dry with a soft towel. Avoid wearing tight-fitting clothes that could rub against the affected area. If the skin is irritated or inflamed, apply a soothing cream or lotion to the area. You may also want to apply a cold compress to help reduce inflammation. If the problem persists or gets worse, consider seeing a dermatologist or healthcare provider for advice on how to best treat the condition.

When will I start to grow chest hair?

Boys typically begin to grow chest hair between the ages of 12 and 14 years old. However, some boys may not develop chest hair until later in puberty, while others may start growing it earlier. The amount and pattern of chest hair growth can vary from person to person and can continue to develop into early adulthood.

FIND OUT MORE!

Here are some of the most helpful:

KidsHealth: This website offers a wide range of information on puberty for boys, including articles on body changes, emotions, hygiene, and more. It also includes a section for parents and caregivers to help them support their child through puberty. Visit: https://kidshealth.org/en/teens/male-puberty.html

TeensHealth: TeensHealth is another great resource for boys going through puberty. It offers articles, videos, and interactive tools on a variety of topics, including body changes, hygiene, and sexual health. The website also includes a section specifically for guys, which covers topics like shaving, voice changes, and acne. Visit: https://teenshealth.org/en/teens/guy-stuff/

The American Academy of Pediatrics: The American Academy of Pediatrics offers a comprehensive guide to puberty for boys, including information on body changes, sexuality, and emotional health. The website also includes a section on what to expect during a doctor's visit and how to talk to a healthcare provider about any concerns.

Visit: https://www.healthychildren.org/English/ages-stages/gradeschool/puberty/Pages/Puberty-What-Parents-Need-to-Know.aspx

Planned Parenthood: Planned Parenthood offers information and resources on sexual health for boys going through puberty. The website includes articles on topics like puberty, anatomy, and contraception, as well as information on how to talk to a healthcare provider about sexual health concerns. Visit: https://www.plannedparenthood.org/learn/teens/puberty/puberty-101

Boys Town National Hotline: Boys Town National Hotline is a free, confidential service that offers support and resources for boys going through puberty. Trained counselors are available 24/7 to provide advice and guidance on a variety of topics, including puberty, mental health, and relationships. Visit: https://www.boystown.org/hotline/Pages/default.aspx

The Trevor Project: The Trevor Project is a national organization that provides crisis intervention and suicide prevention services to LGBTQ+ youth. The website offers resources and support for boys going through puberty who may be questioning their sexual orientation or gender identity. Visit: https://www.thetrevorproject.org/

Center for Young Men's Health: The Center for Young Men's Health is a website designed specifically for teenage boys. It includes information on puberty, sexual health, and mental health, as well as tips on healthy living and relationships. The website also offers a forum where boys can ask questions and get advice from healthcare providers. Visit: https://youngmenshealthsite.org/

GLOSSARY

Acne: A skin condition caused by clogged hair follicles, resulting in pimples, blackheads, and whiteheads.

Androgens: Male hormones produced in the testes, adrenal glands, and ovaries. They promote the development of male characteristics during puberty.

Deodorant: A product used to prevent body odor caused by the bacterial breakdown of sweat.

Ejaculation: The release of semen from the penis during sexual climax.

Grooming: The act of maintaining one's personal hygiene and appearance.

Hormones: Chemical messengers produced by the endocrine glands that regulate bodily functions, including puberty.

Masturbation: Sexual self-stimulation that leads to orgasm.

Penis: Male sex organ used for urination and sexual reproduction.

Puberty: The period of physical and emotional development during which a child matures into an adult capable of reproduction.

Pubic hair: Hair that grows around the genitals during puberty.

Razor burn: Irritation and redness of the skin caused by shaving.

Scrotum: The sac of skin that contains the testes.

Semen: The fluid that is ejaculated from the penis during orgasm and contains sperm.

Shaving: The act of removing hair from the skin using a razor or electric shaver.

Testes: The male reproductive organs that produce sperm and testosterone.

Testosterone: The male hormone responsible for the development of male characteristics during puberty.

Underarm hair: Hair that grows in the armpits during puberty.

Wet dream: A spontaneous orgasm that occurs during sleep.

Whiteheads: Small, white bumps on the skin caused by clogged hair follicles.

Yeast infection: An infection caused by the overgrowth of yeast on the skin, resulting in itching, redness, and discomfort.

Zits: Slang term for pimples, which are raised red bumps on the skin caused by clogged hair follicles.

INDEX

Made in the USA
Coppell, TX
04 June 2023

17669019R00079